AF380011

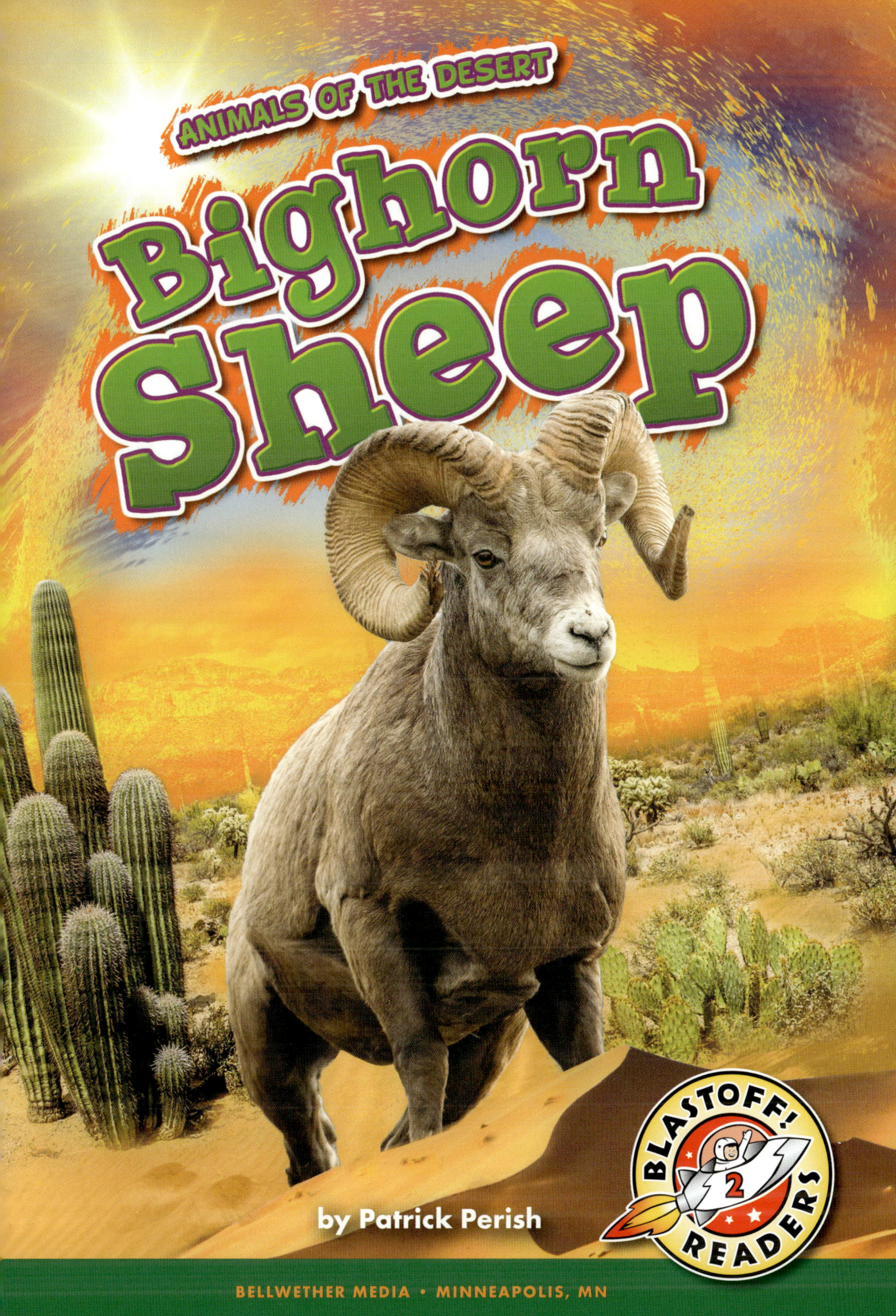

ANIMALS OF THE DESERT
Bighorn Sheep
by Patrick Perish
BLASTOFF! READERS
2
BELLWETHER MEDIA • MINNEAPOLIS, MN

Note to Librarians, Teachers, and Parents:

Blastoff! Readers are carefully developed by literacy experts and combine standards-based content with developmentally appropriate text.

Level 1 provides the most support through repetition of high-frequency words, light text, predictable sentence patterns, and strong visual support.

Level 2 offers early readers a bit more challenge through varied simple sentences, increased text load, and less repetition of high-frequency words.

Level 3 advances early-fluent readers toward fluency through increased text and concept load, less reliance on visuals, longer sentences, and more literary language.

Level 4 builds reading stamina by providing more text per page, increased use of punctuation, greater variation in sentence patterns, and increasingly challenging vocabulary.

Level 5 encourages children to move from "learning to read" to "reading to learn" by providing even more text, varied writing styles, and less familiar topics.

Whichever book is right for your reader, Blastoff! Readers are the perfect books to build confidence and encourage a love of reading that will last a lifetime!

This edition first published in 2019 by Bellwether Media, Inc.

Library of Congress Cataloging-in-Publication Data

Names: Perish, Patrick, author.
Title: Bighorn Sheep / by Patrick Perish.
Description: Minneapolis, MN : Bellwether Media, Inc., 2019. | Series:
  Blastoff! Readers. Animals of the Desert | Audience: Age 5-8. | Audience:
  K to Grade 3. | Includes bibliographical references and index.
Identifiers: LCCN 2018030995 (print) | LCCN 2018037392 (ebook) | ISBN
  9781681036311 (ebook) | ISBN 9781626179202 (hardcover : alk. paper)
Subjects: LCSH: Bighorn sheep--Juvenile literature. | Desert animals--Juvenile literature.
Classification: LCC QL737.U53 (ebook) | LCC QL737.U53 P386 2019 (print) | DDC
  599.649/7--dc23
LC record available at https://lccn.loc.gov/2018030995

Editor: Rebecca Sabelko   Designer: Josh Brink

Printed in the United States of America, North Mankato, MN

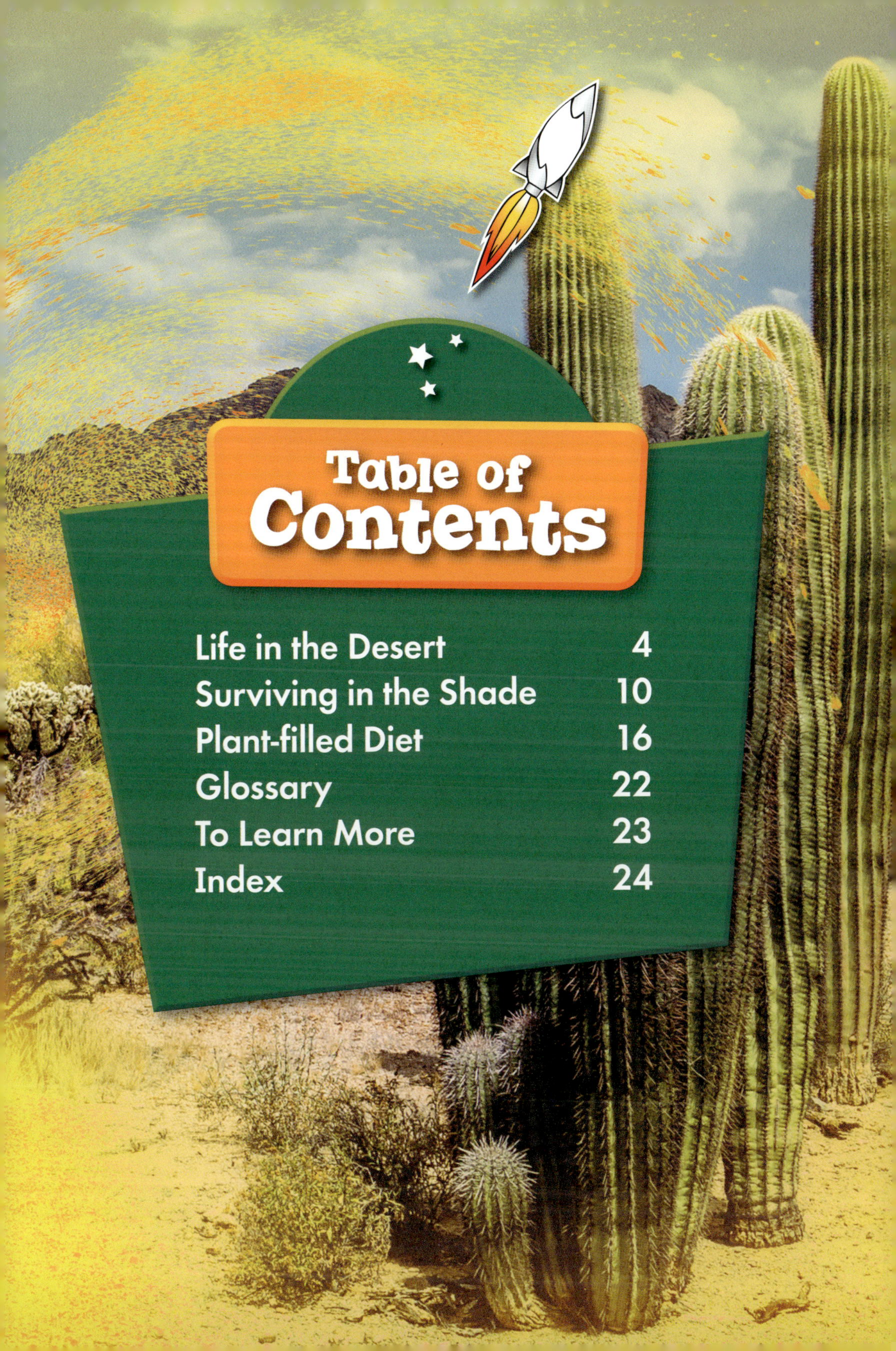

Table of Contents

Life in the Desert

Desert bighorn sheep live
in the deserts of the
southwestern United States
and northern Mexico.

They are built for this hot
and rocky **biome**.

Desert Bighorn Sheep Range

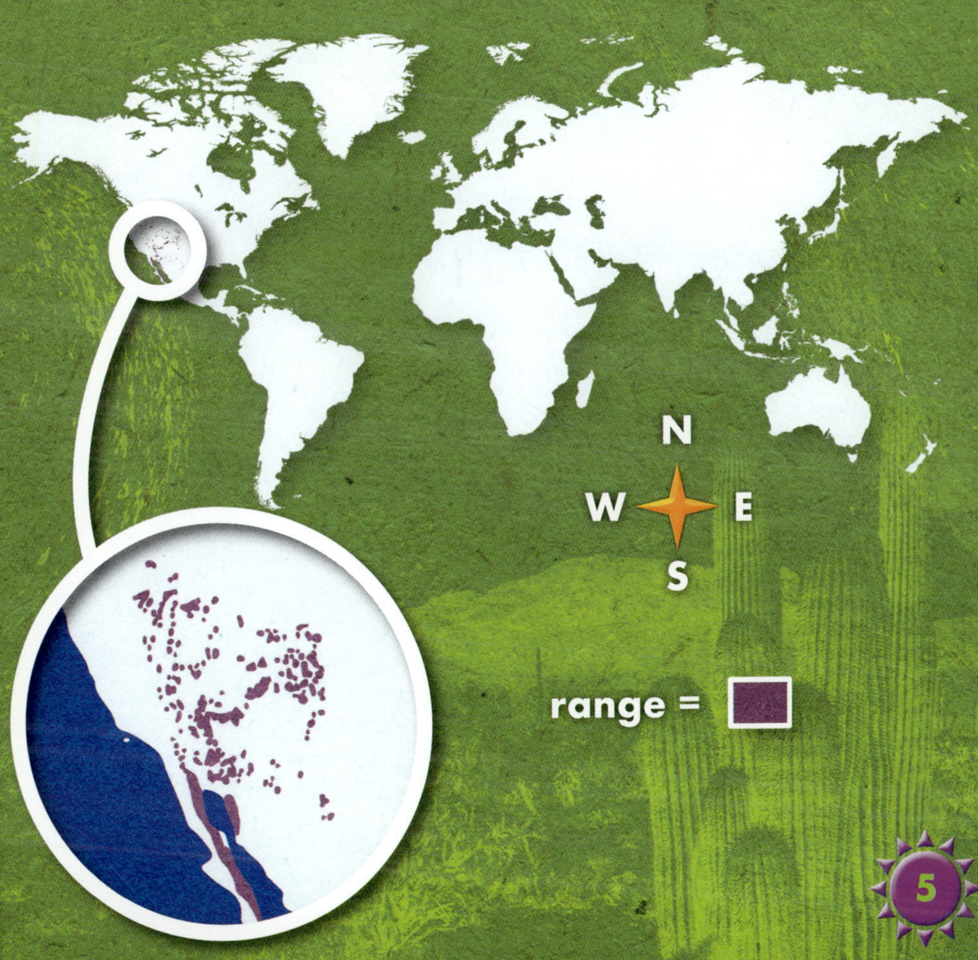

Bighorns have good eyesight. They can spot **predators** many miles away.

Their padded **split hooves** let them easily climb rough ground to escape.

These sheep have **adapted** to the dry desert.

Special Adaptations

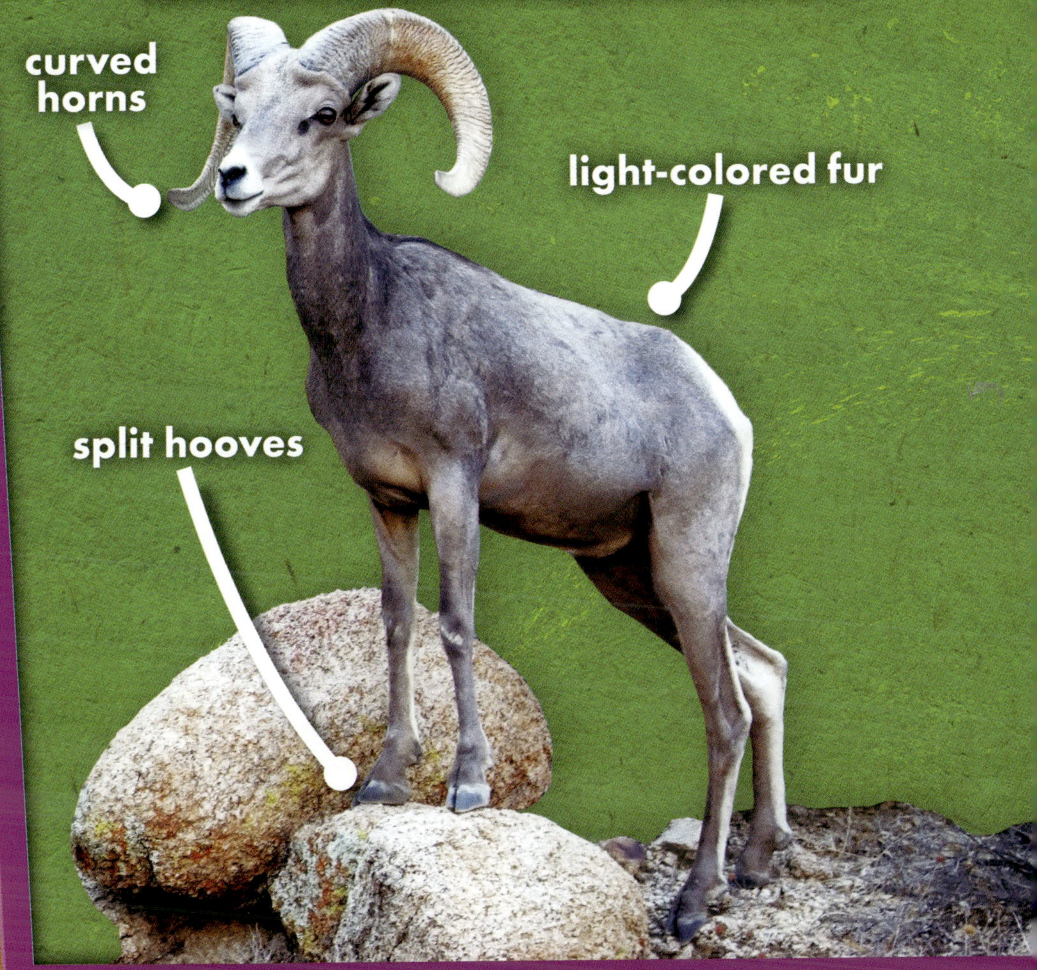

Their bodies get the most out of their food. They do not waste anything!

Surviving in the Shade

Desert bighorns keep cool
by panting and sweating.

Their light brown fur
reflects sunlight
to keep them cool, too!

11

Bighorn sheep often rest during the hottest parts of the day.

They find shade under cliffs or in caves.

Desert bighorns drink a lot of water at one time. They can go days without water.

This helps the bighorns
survive dry spells.

15

Plant-filled Diet

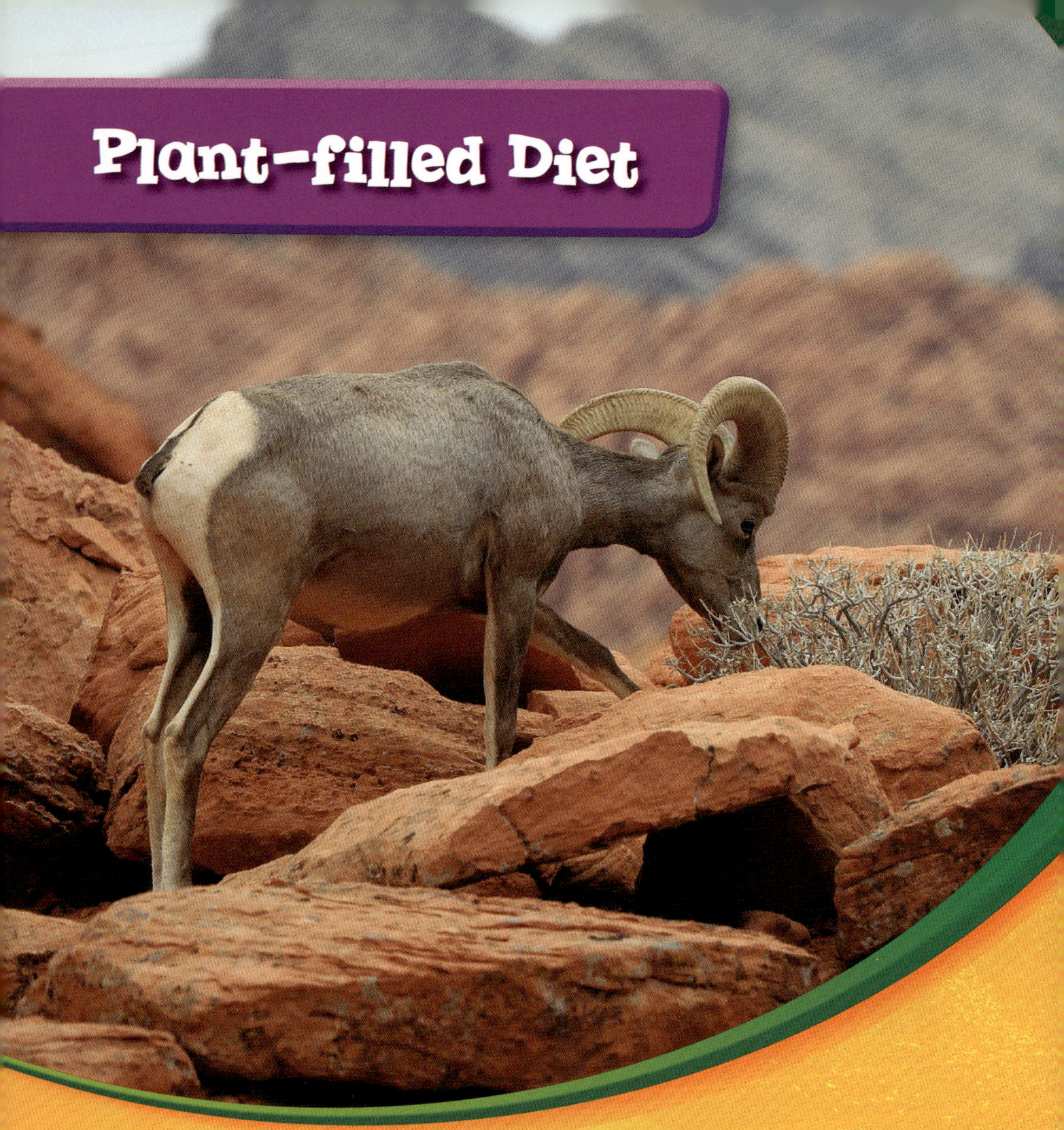

Bighorns get much of their water from the food they eat. They eat shrubs and grasses.

Their favorite foods are
desert wildflowers.

Bighorn Sheep Diet

Bighorn sheep even eat cacti. They rub the **spines** off with their horns.

Then, they break the cacti open and drink the juices.

Bighorn Sheep Stats

Least Concern
Near Threatened
Vulnerable
Endangered
Critically Endangered
Extinct in the Wild
Extinct

conservation status: least concern
life span: up to 15 years

19

Mountain deserts are rocky and dry. Bighorns are right at home in this harsh **habitat**.

20

They are true desert survivors!

Glossary

adapted—changed over a long period of time

biome—a large area with certain plants, animals, and weather

habitat—land with certain types of plants, animals, and weather

predators—animals that hunt other animals for food

reflects—throws back heat and light

spines—sharp, pointed parts of some plants or animals

split hooves—hooves that are split into two toes; hooves are hard coverings that protect the feet of some animals.

To Learn More

AT THE LIBRARY

Gagne, Tammy. *Bighorn Sheep*. Lake Elmo, Minn.: Focus Readers, 2017.

Loh-Hagan Edd, Virginia. *Bighorn Sheep*. Ann Arbor, Mich.: Cherry Lake Publishing, 2018.

Riggs, Kate. *Bighorn Sheep*. Mankato, Minn.: Creative Education, 2017.

ON THE WEB

FACTSURFER

Factsurfer.com gives you a safe, fun way to find more information.

1. Go to www.factsurfer.com.

2. Enter "bighorn sheep" into the search box.

3. Click the "Surf" button and select your book cover to see a list of related web sites

With factsurfer.com, finding more information is just a click away.

Index